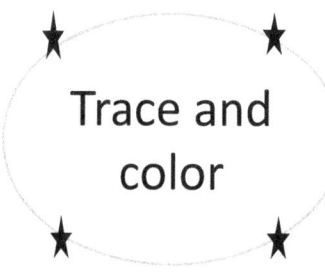

Trace and color

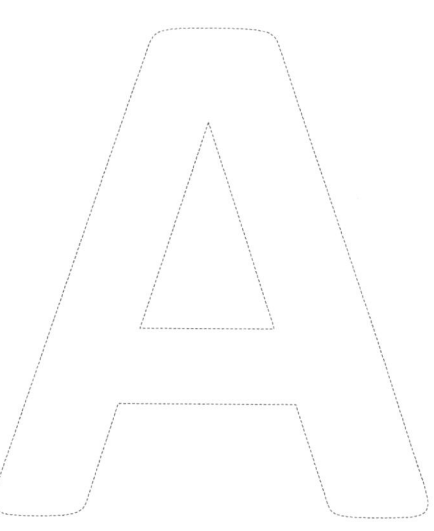

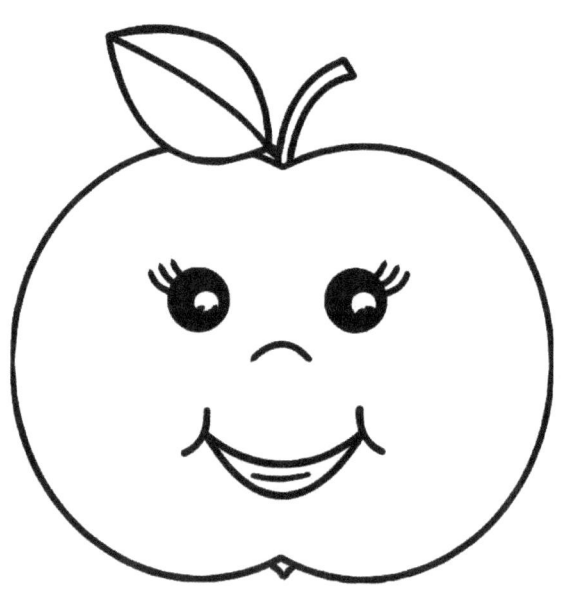

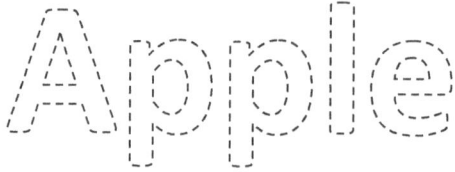

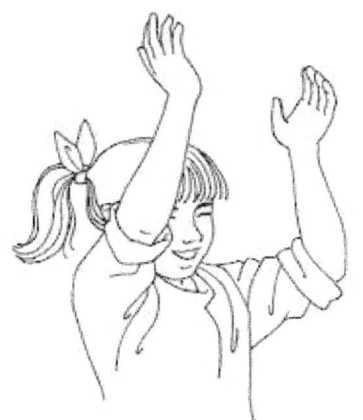

Redraw and color

Trace and color

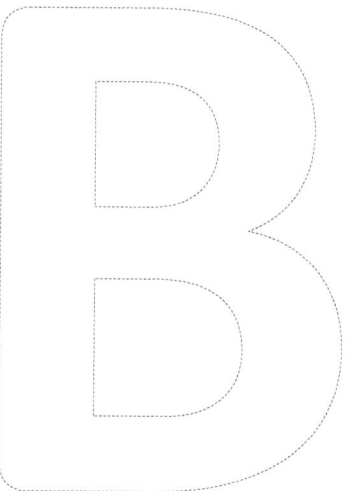

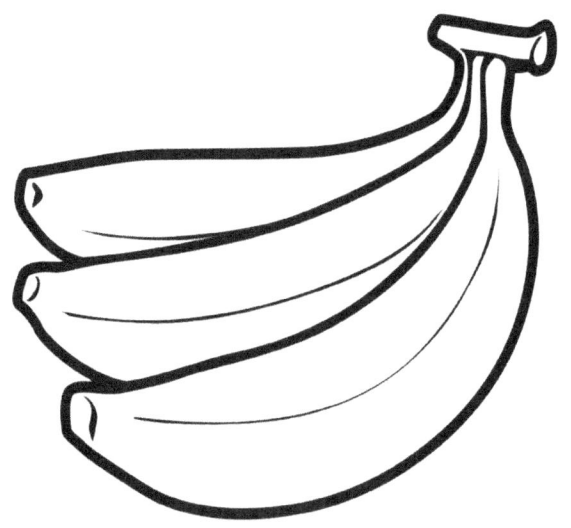

Banana

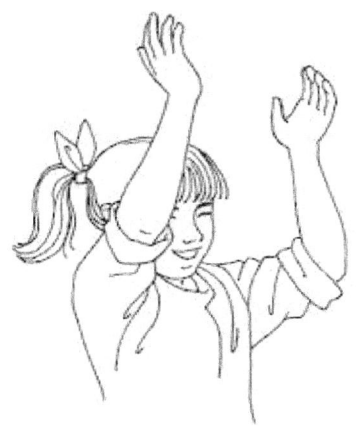

Redraw and color

Trace and
color

C

Cherry

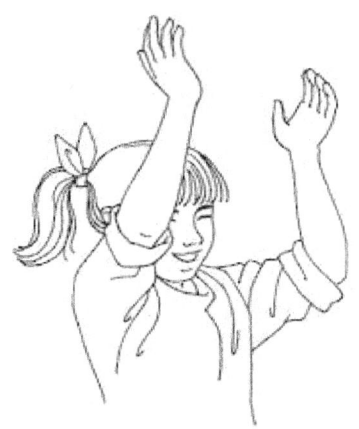

Redraw and color

D

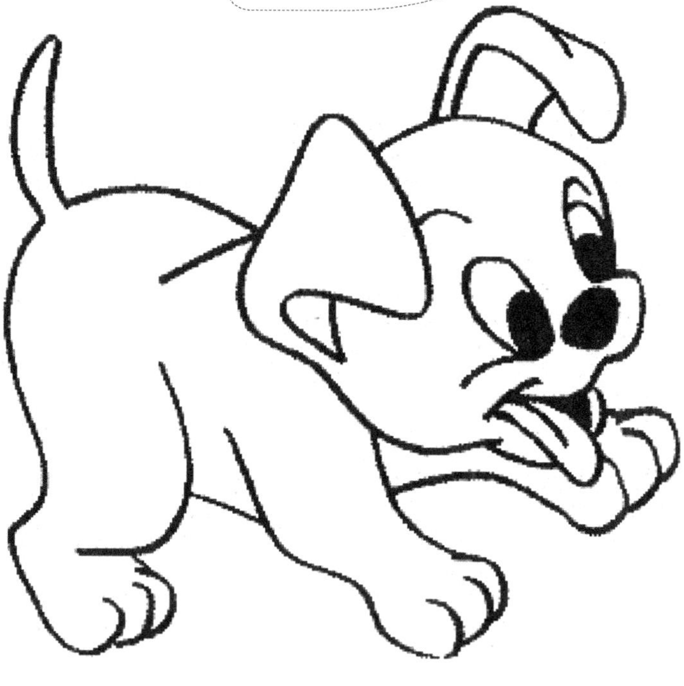

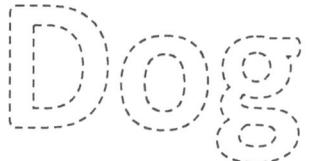

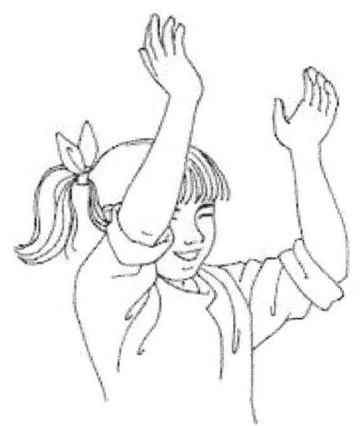

Redraw and color

Trace and color

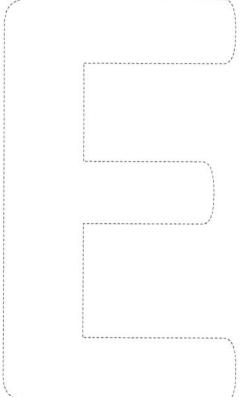

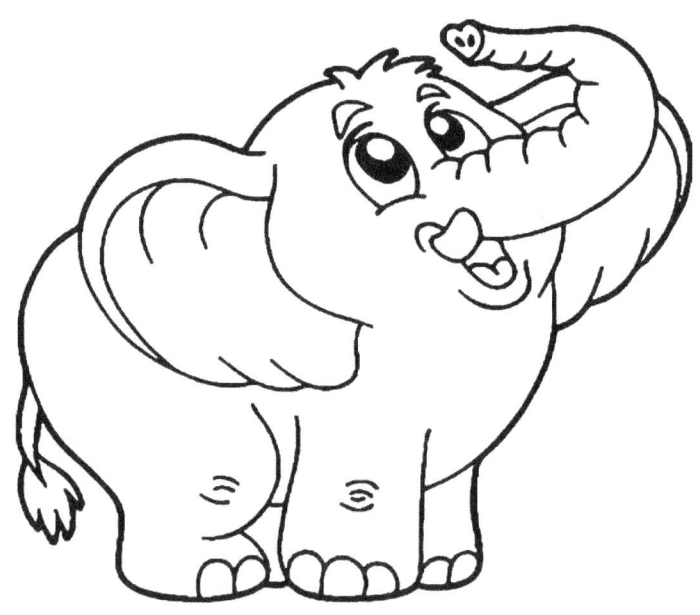

Elephant

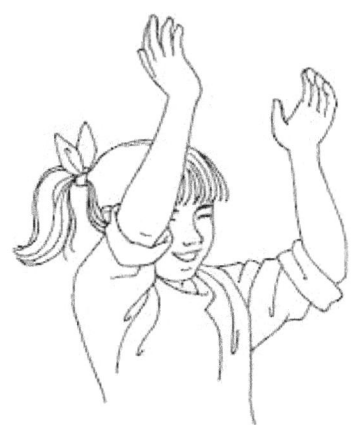

Redraw and color

Trace and color

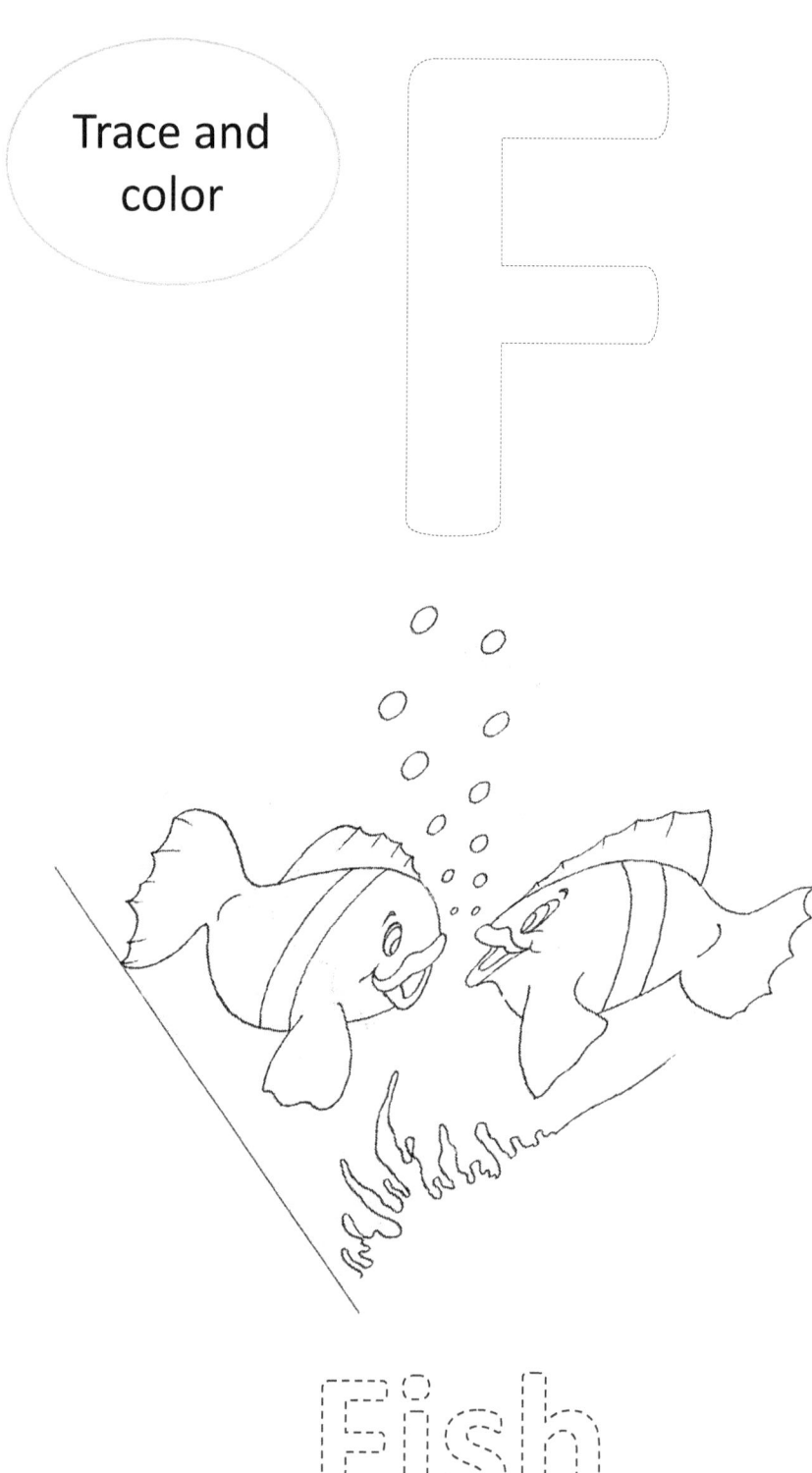

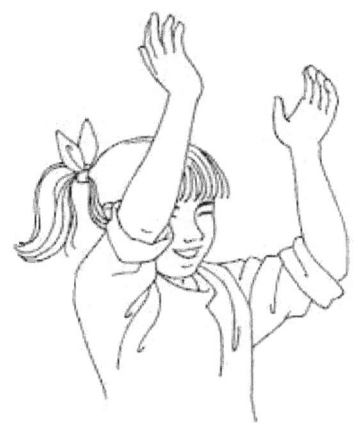

Redraw and color

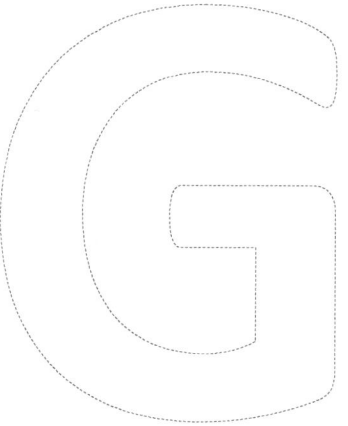

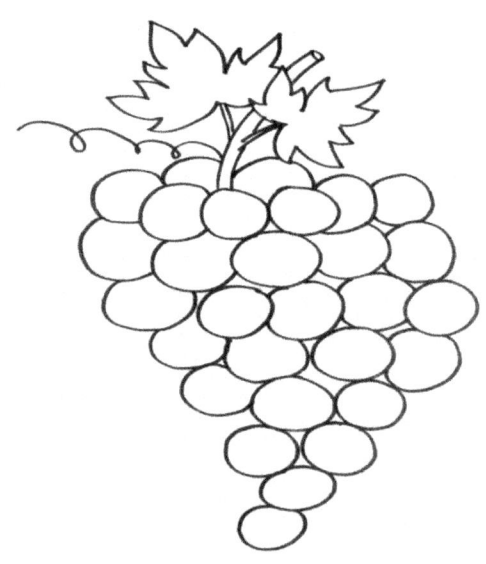

Grapes

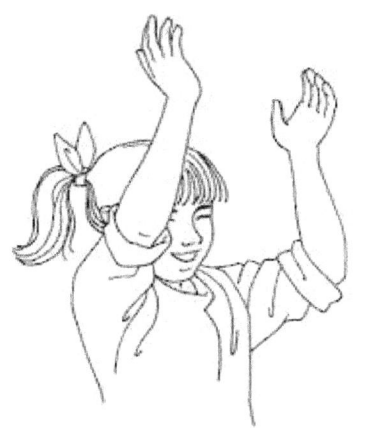

Redraw and color

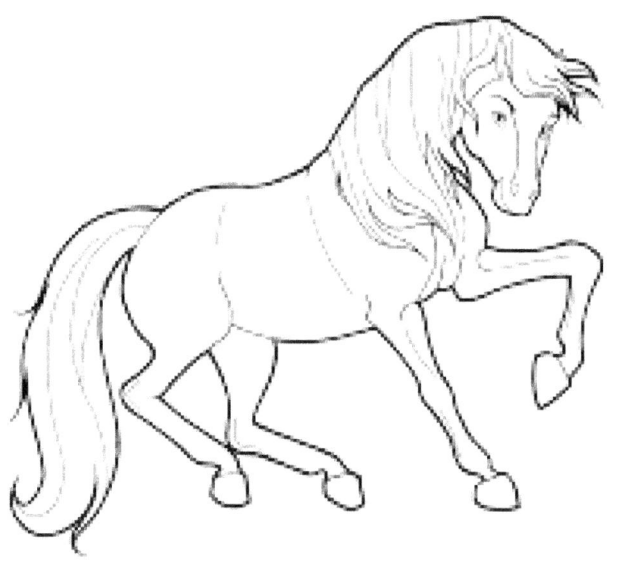

Horse

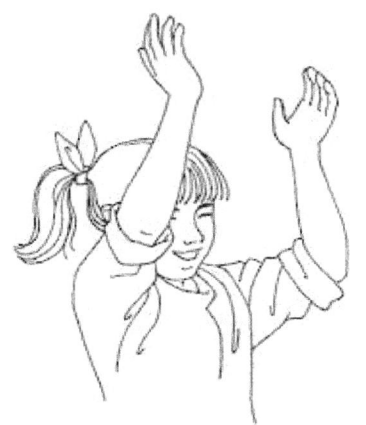

Redraw and color

Trace and
color

I

Ice cream

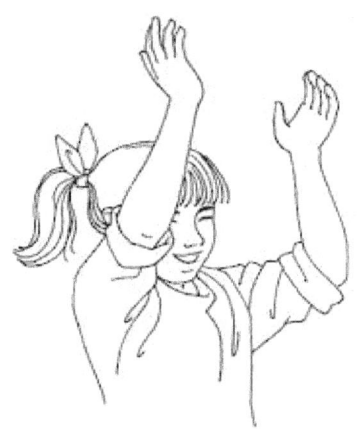

Redraw and color

J

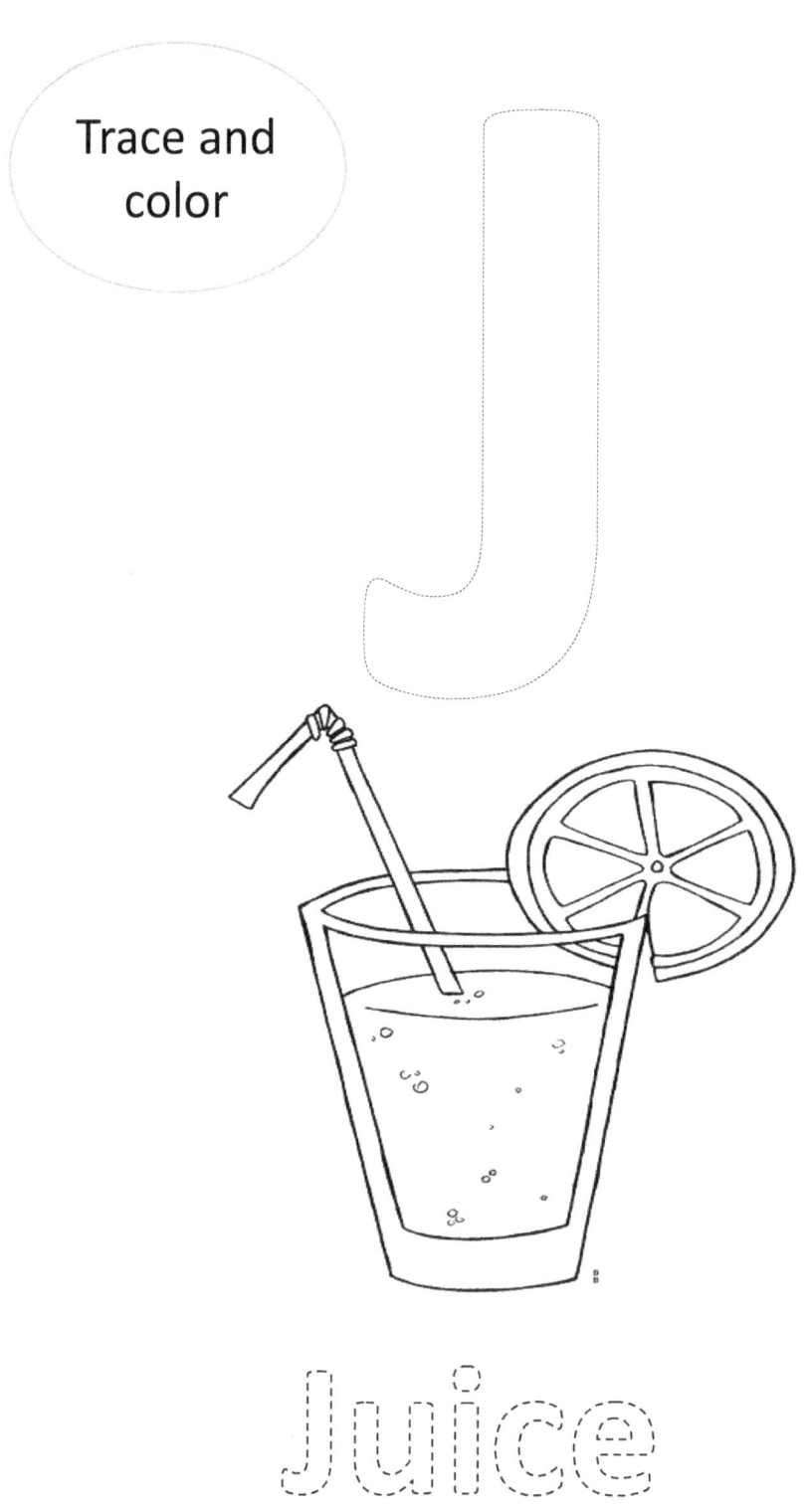

Juice

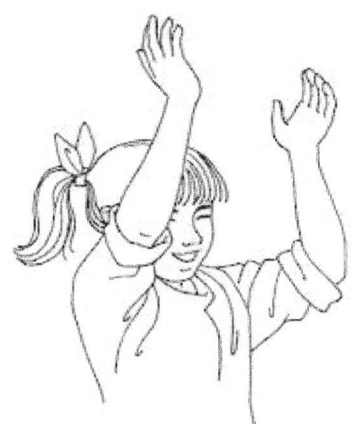

Redraw and color

K

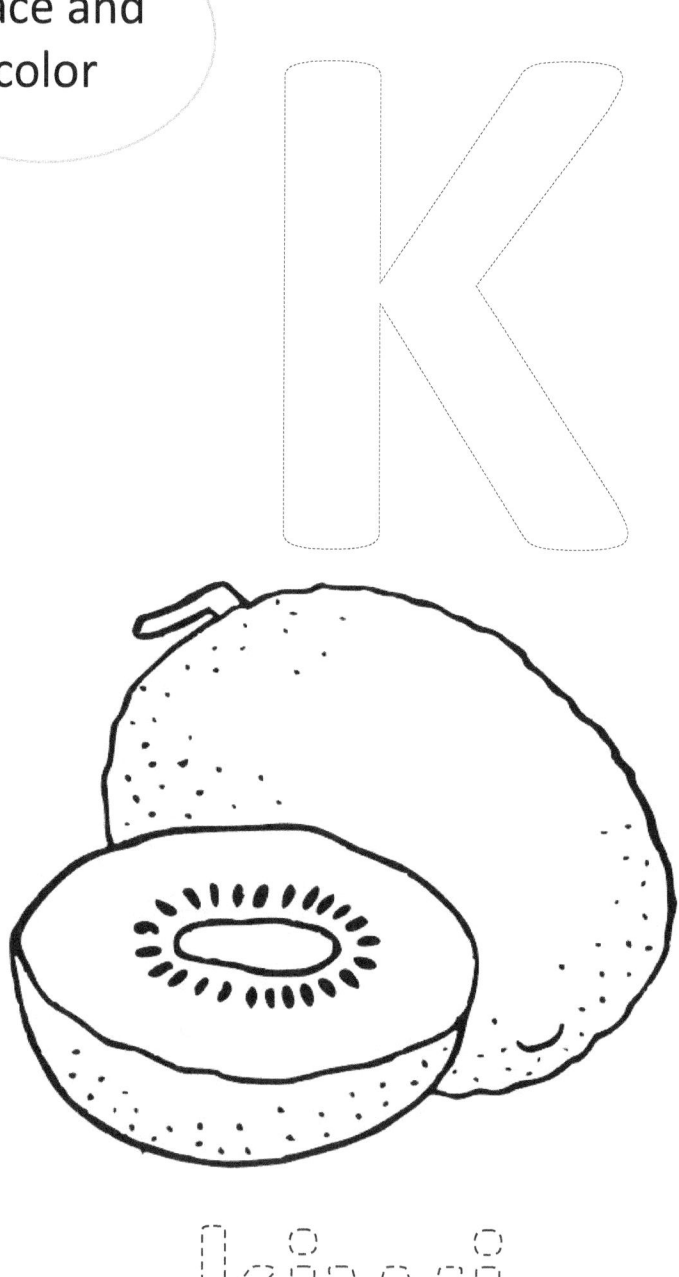

kiwi

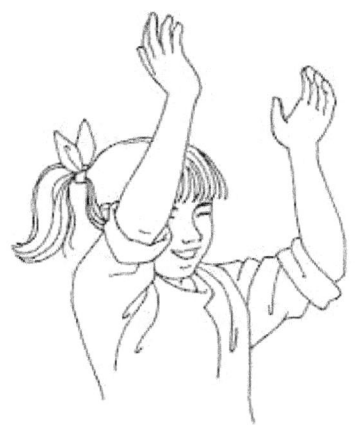

Redraw and color

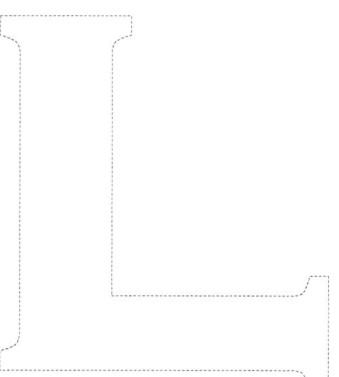

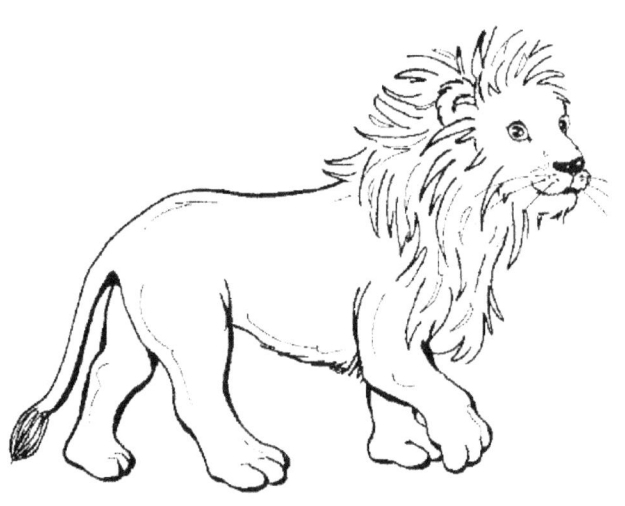

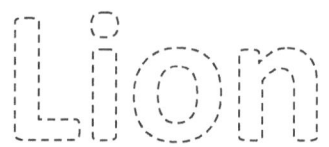

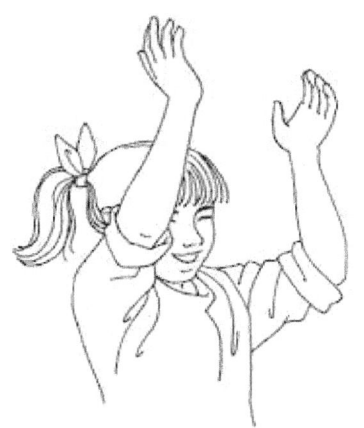

Redraw and color

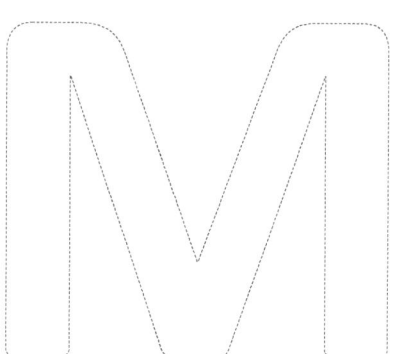

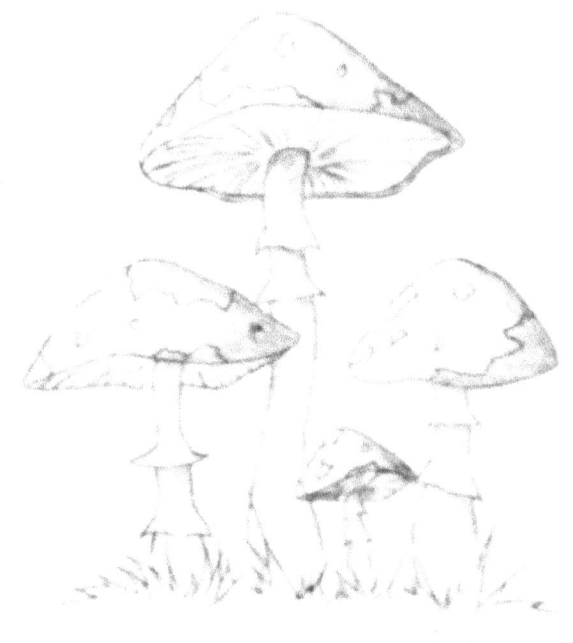

Mushroom

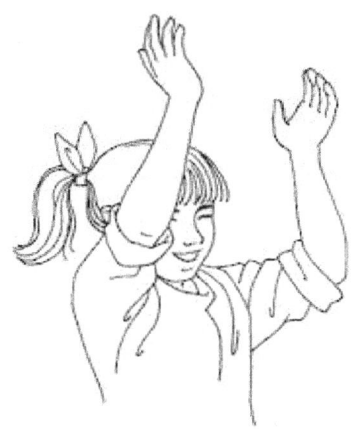

Redraw and color

N

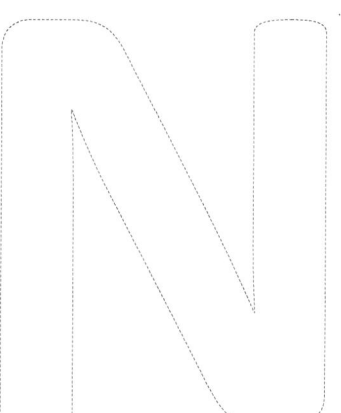

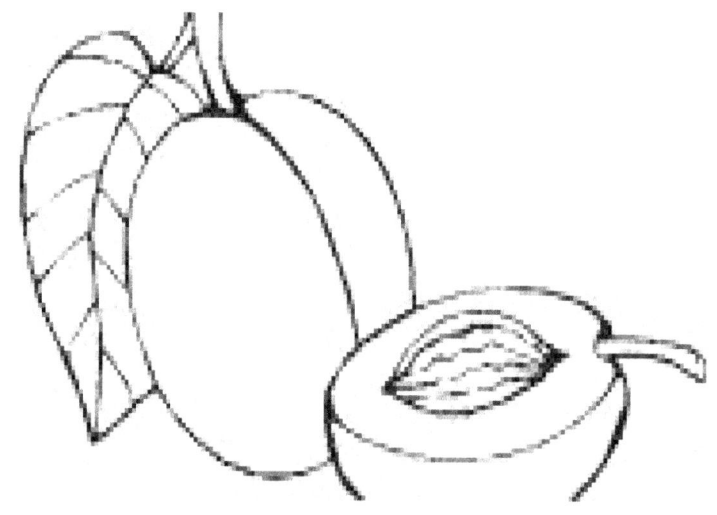

Nectarine

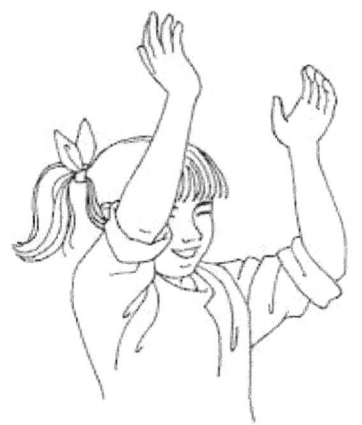

Redraw and color

Trace and
color

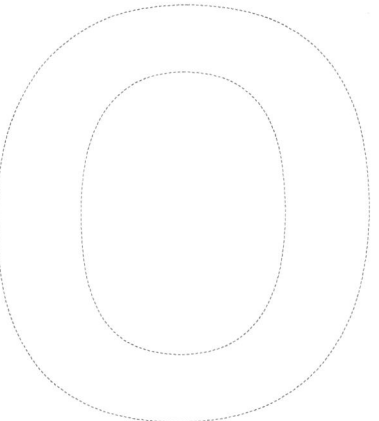

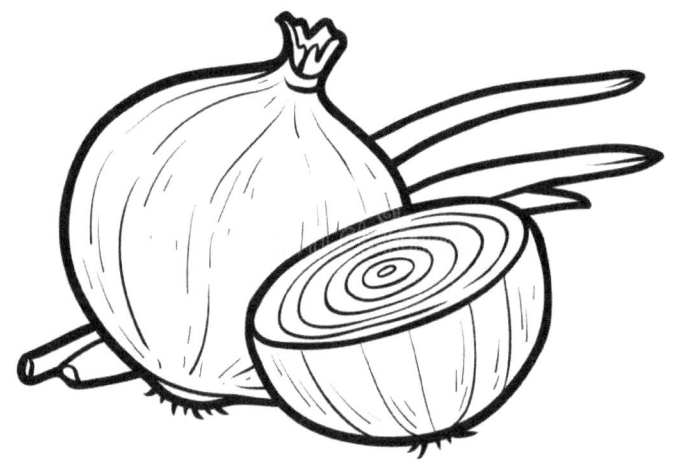

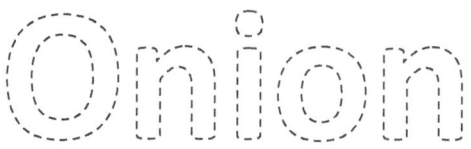

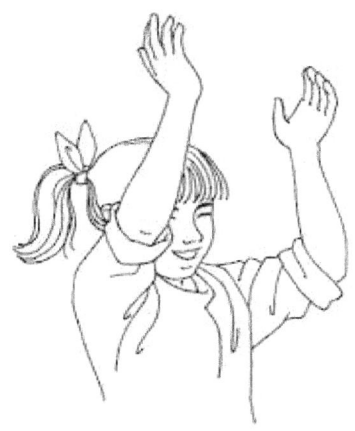

Redraw and color

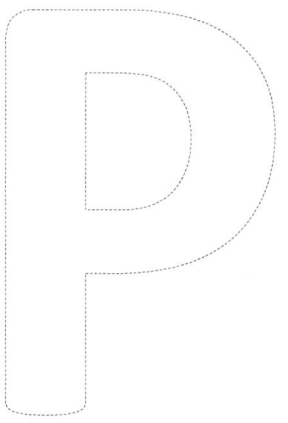

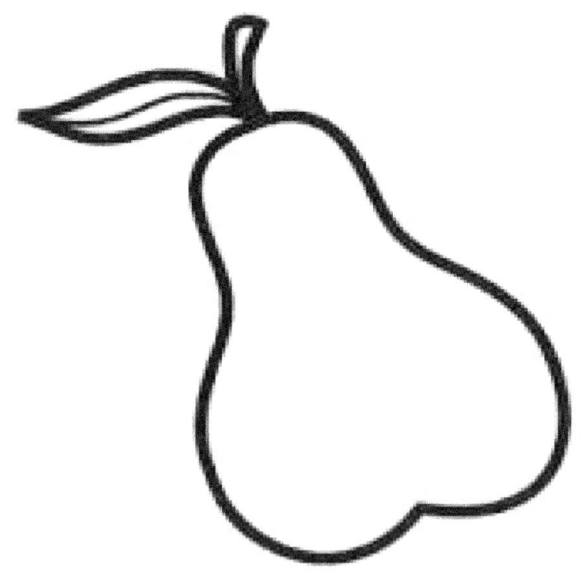

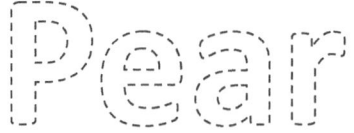

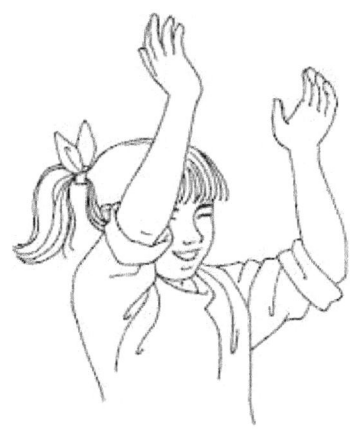

Redraw and color

Q

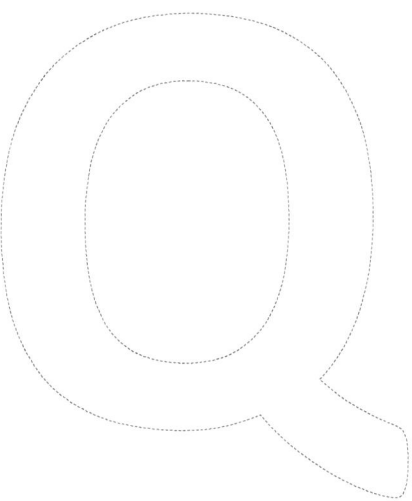

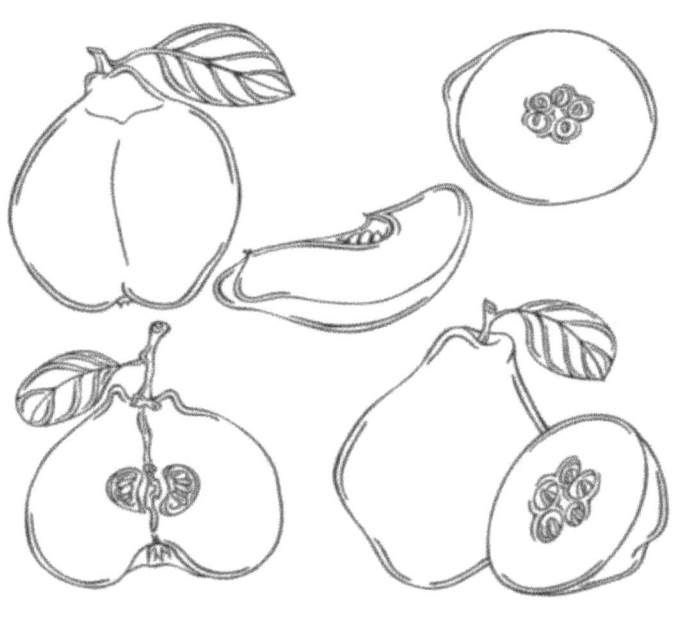

Quince

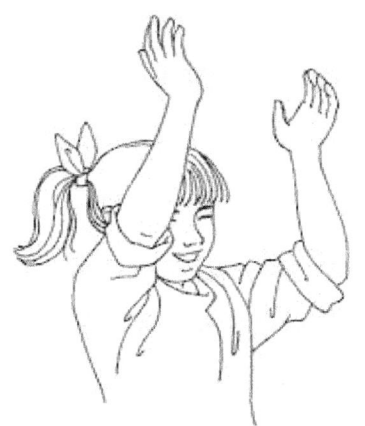

Redraw and color

Trace and color

R

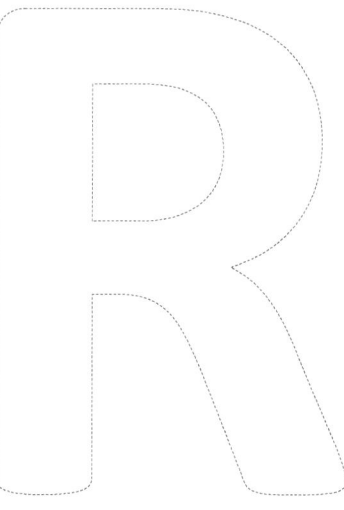

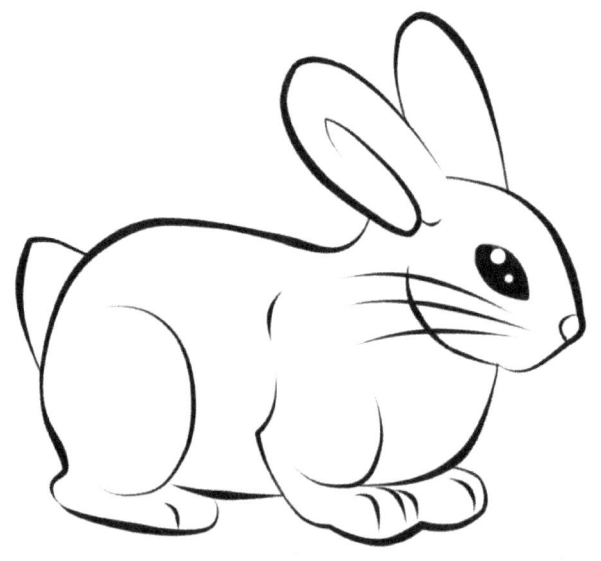

Rabbit

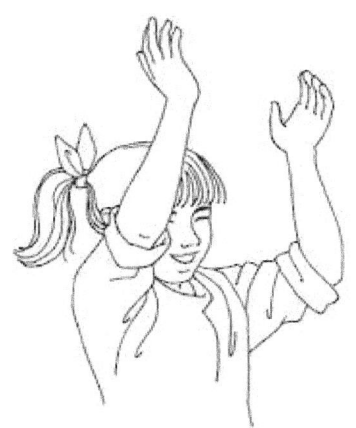

Redraw and color

Trace and color

S

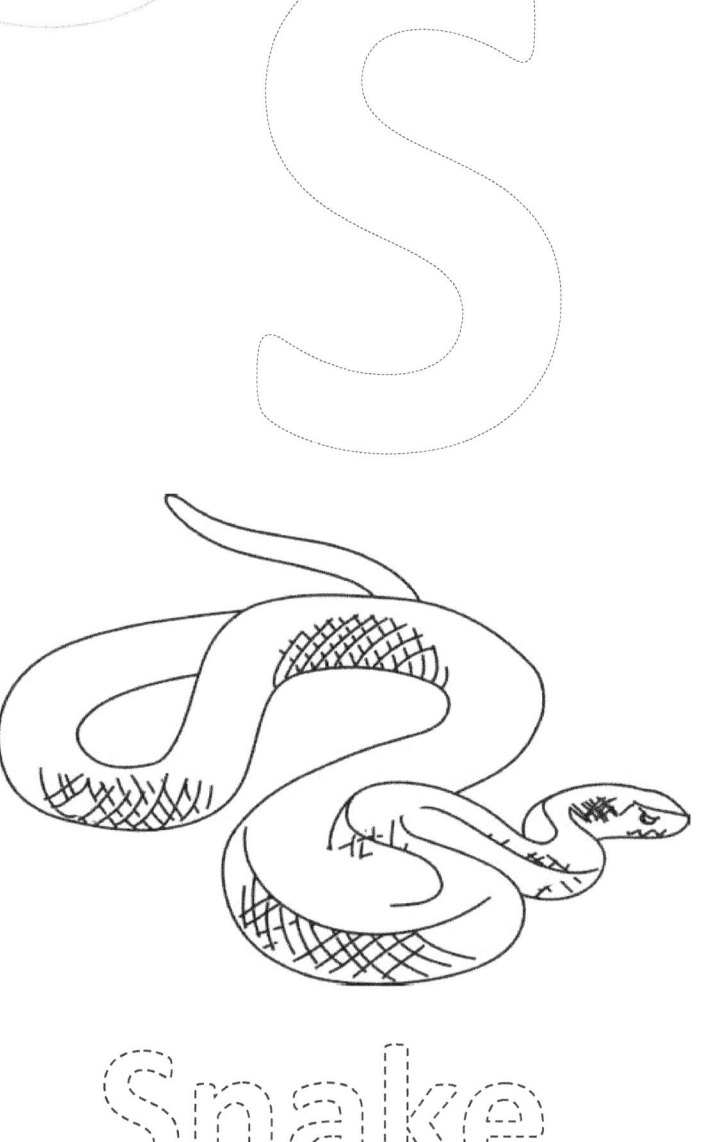

Snake

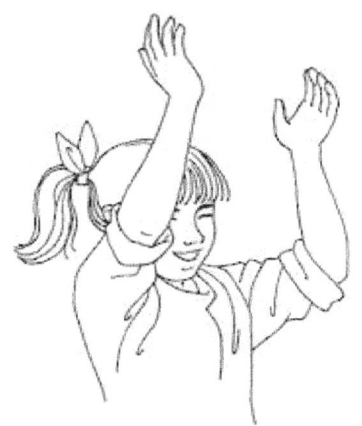

Redraw and color

T

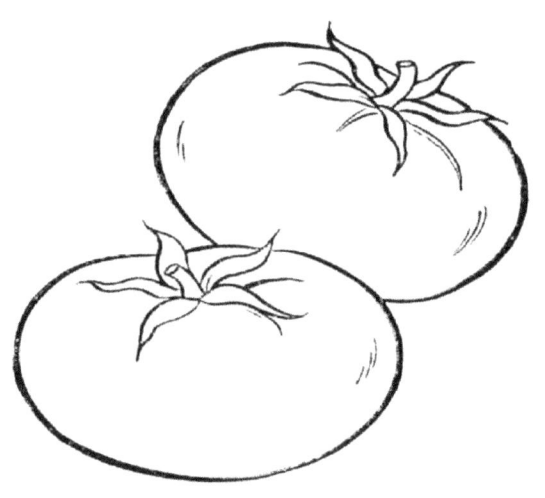

Tomato

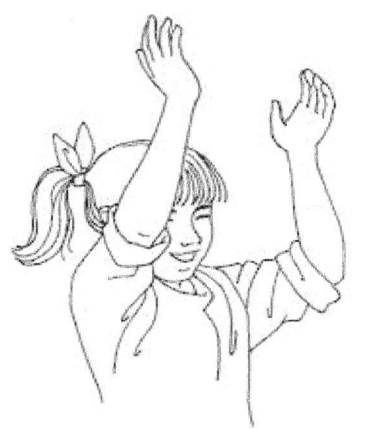

Redraw and color

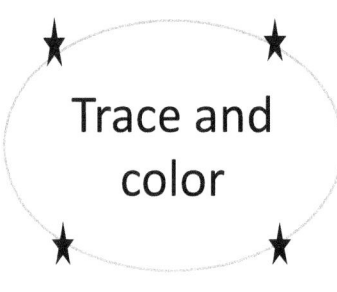

Trace and color

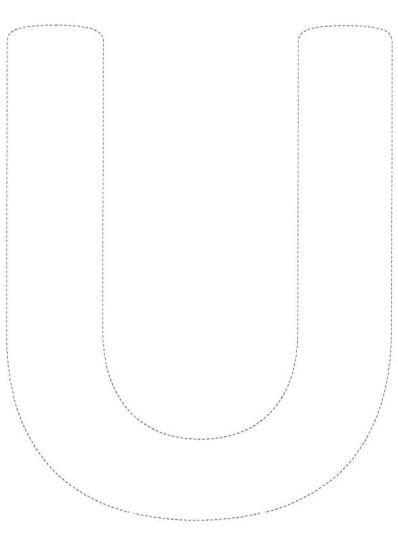

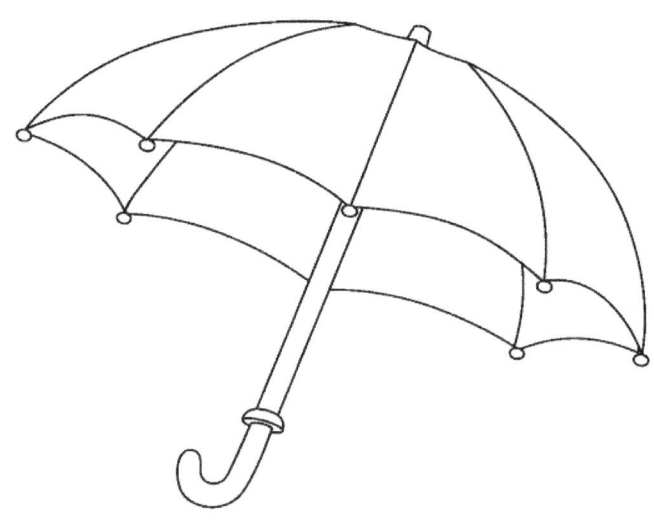

Umbrella

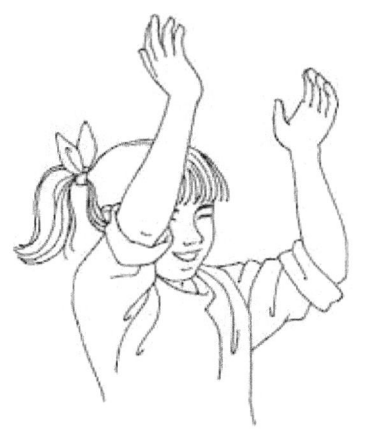

Redraw and color

V

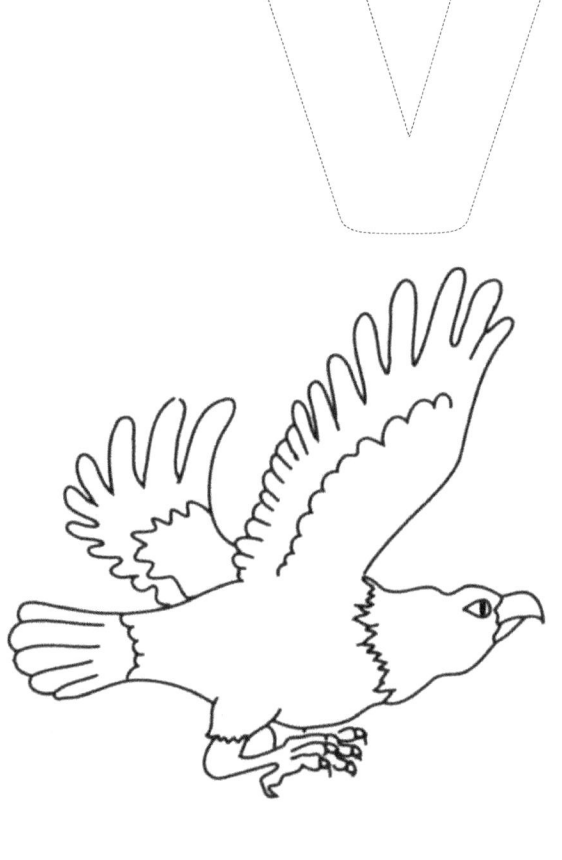

Vulture

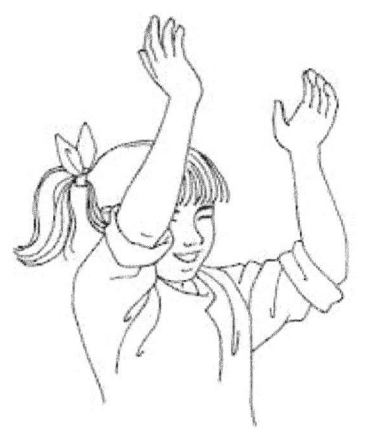

Redraw and color

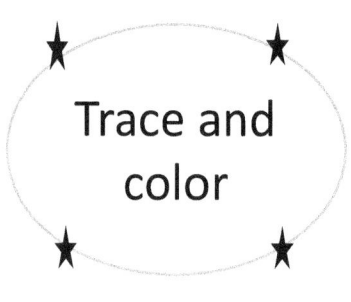

Trace and color

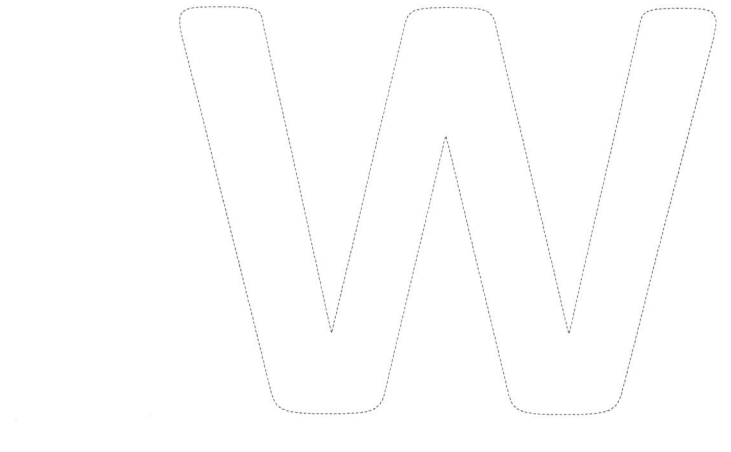

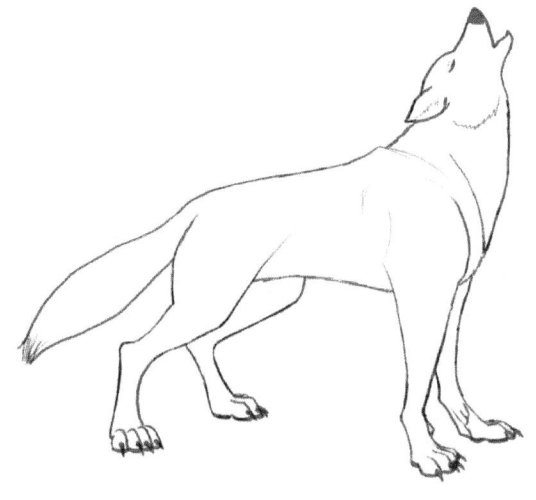

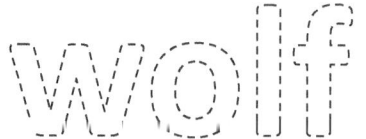

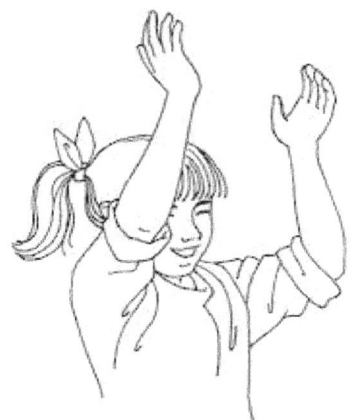

Redraw and color

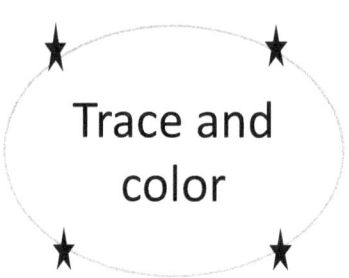

Trace and color

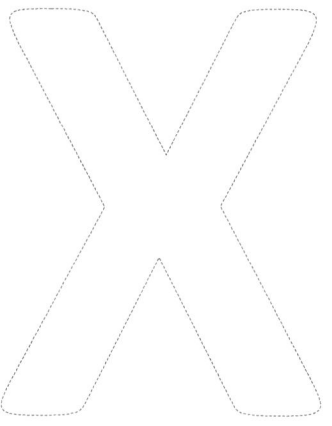

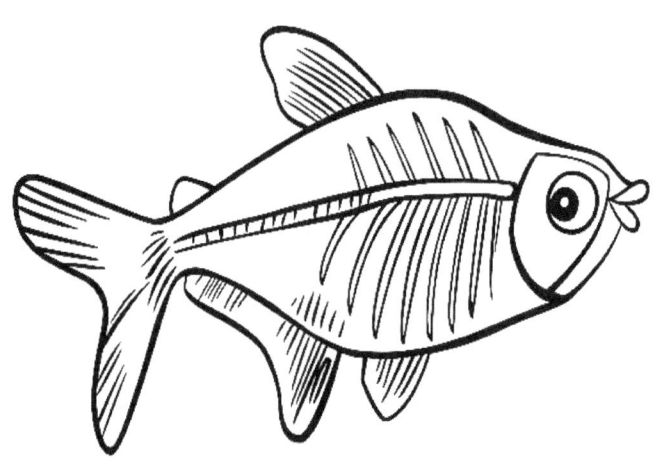

X-ray tetra

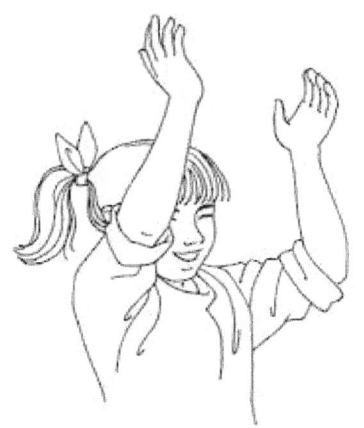

Redraw and color

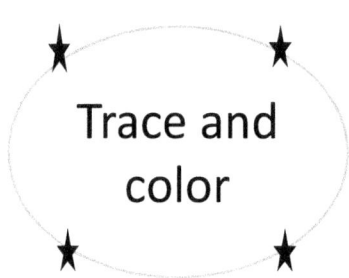
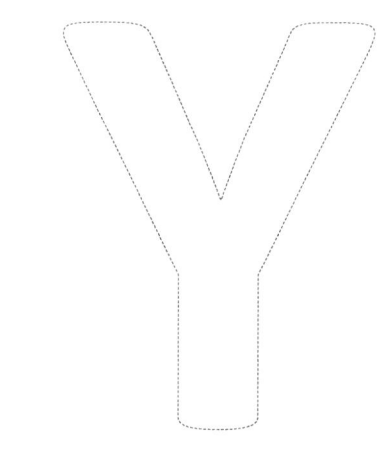

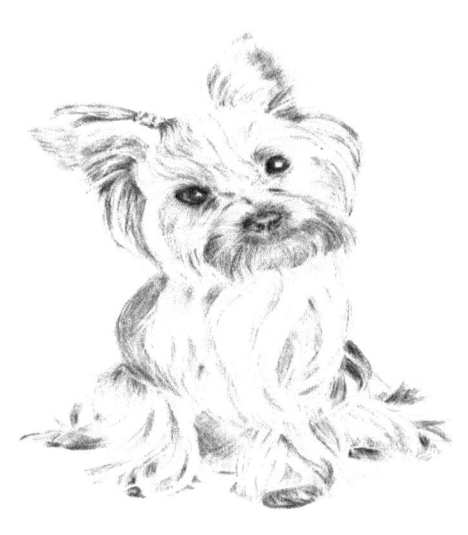

Yorkshire

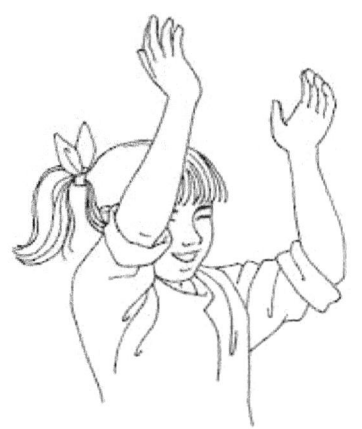

Redraw and color

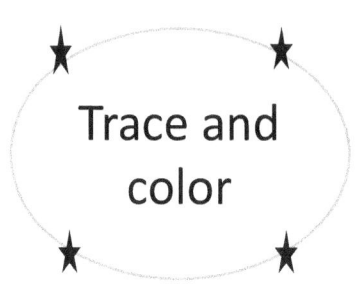

Trace and color

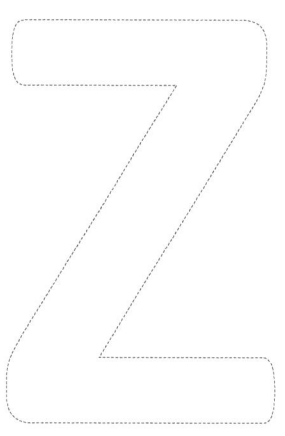

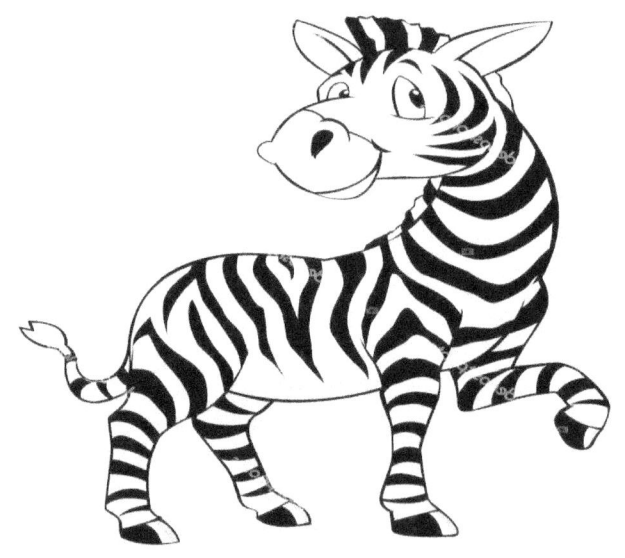

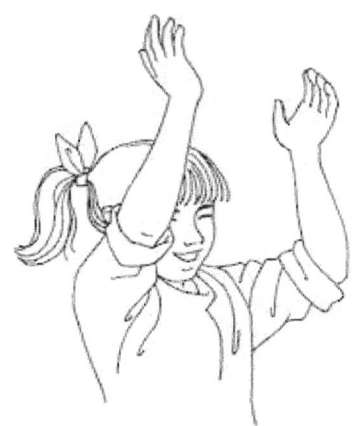

Redraw and color

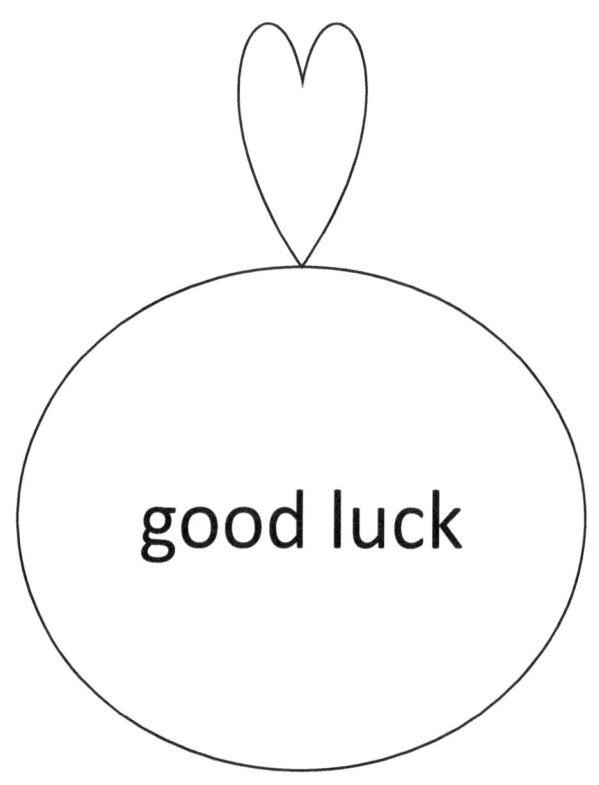

good luck

www.ingramcontent.com/pod-product-compliance
Lightning Source LLC
Chambersburg PA
CBHW071112220526
45467CB00004B/1824